A postcard for you
to color and mail.

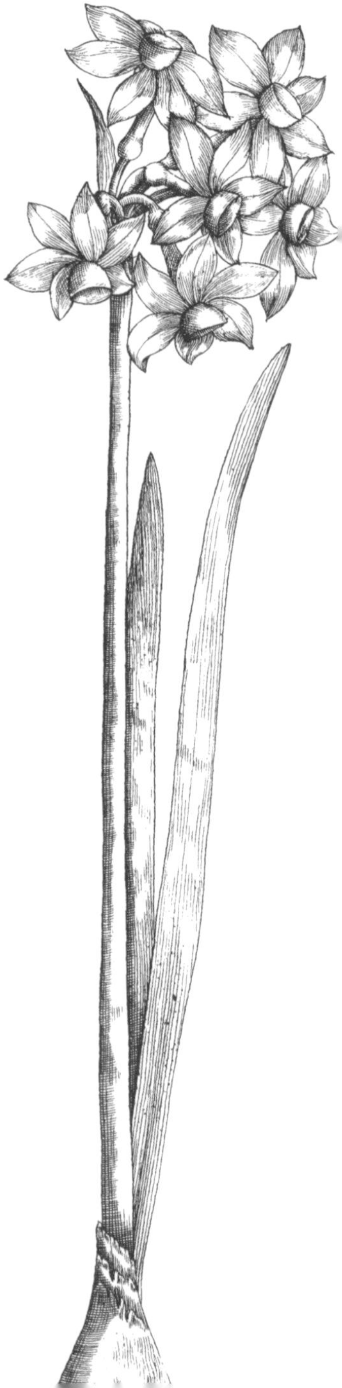

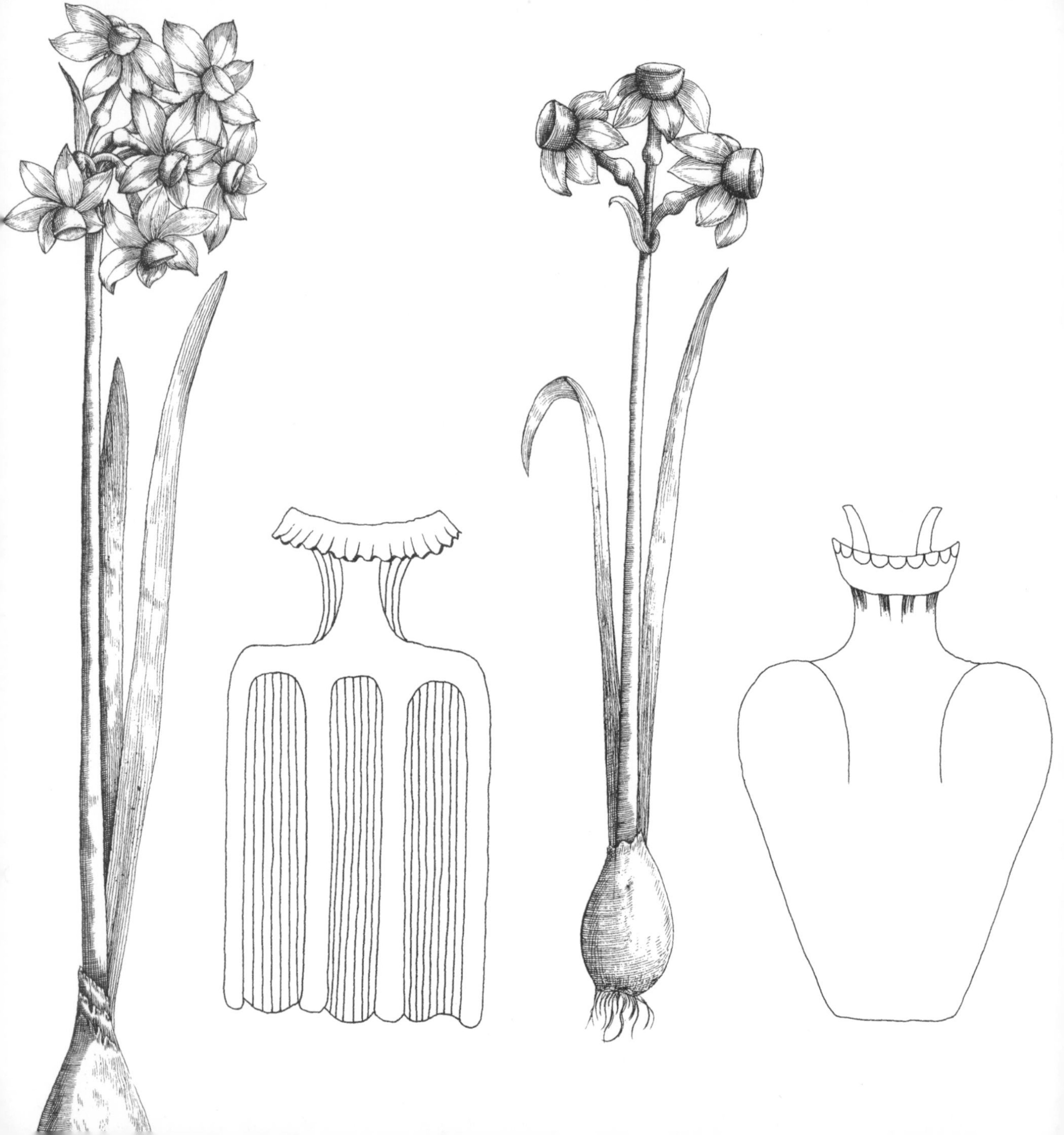

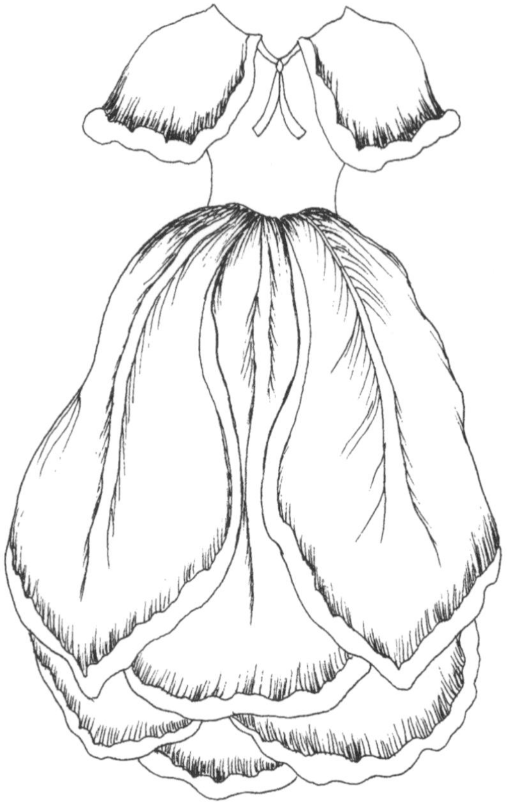

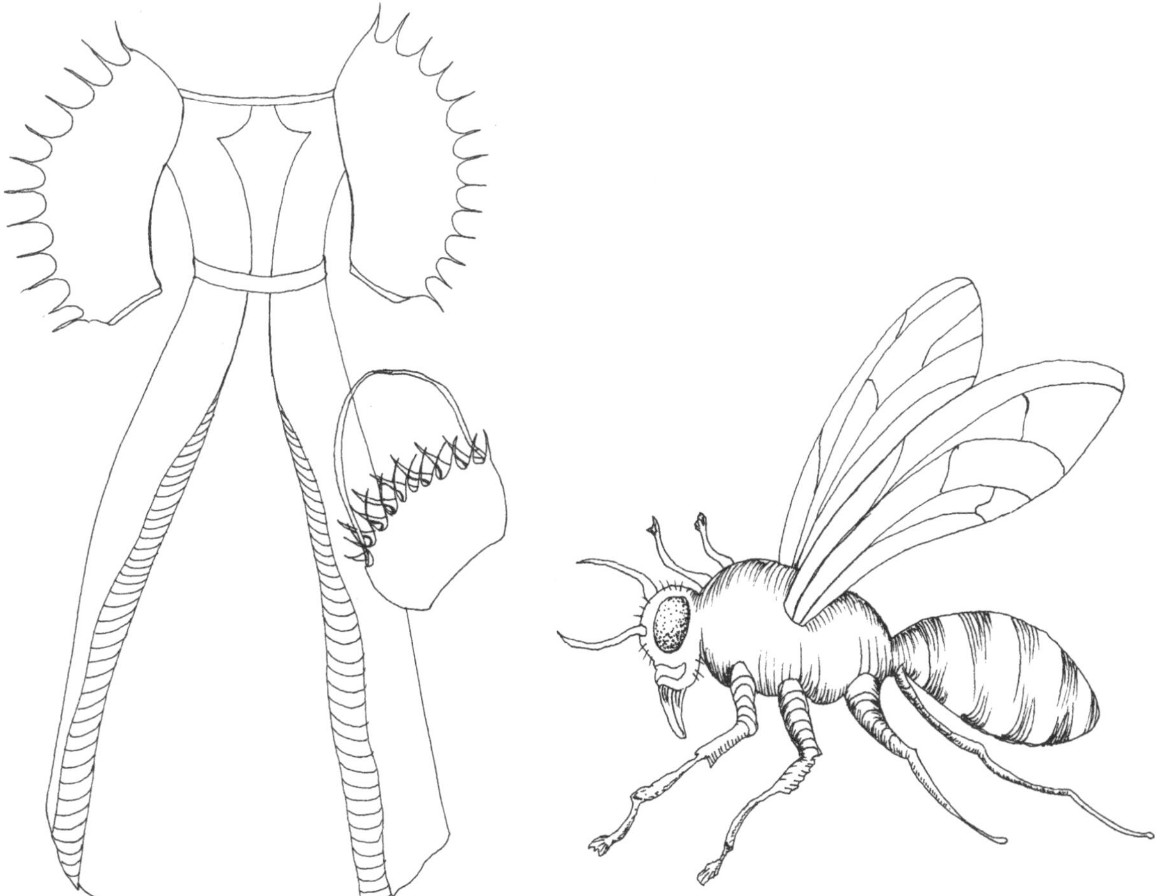

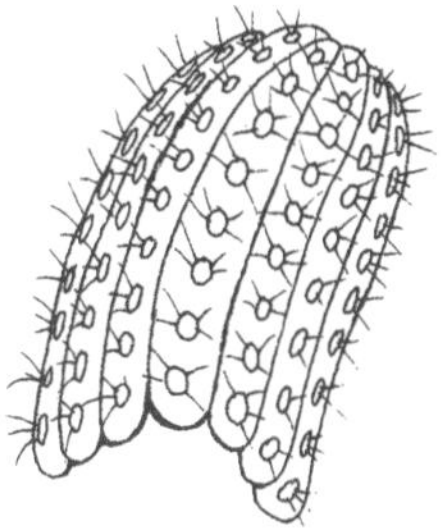

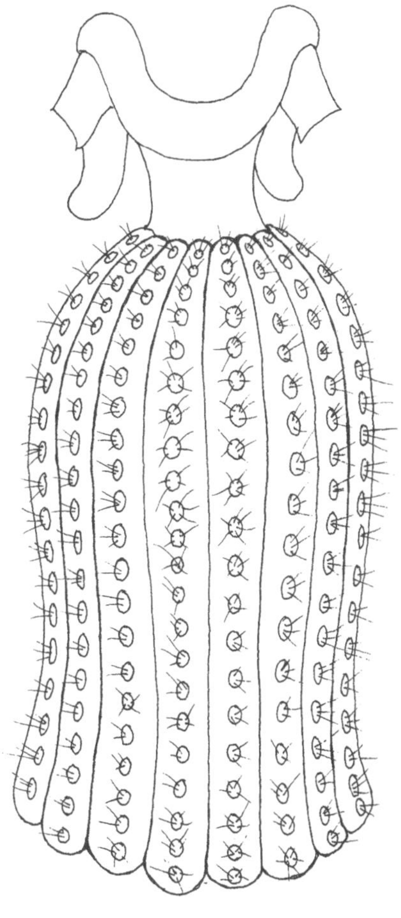

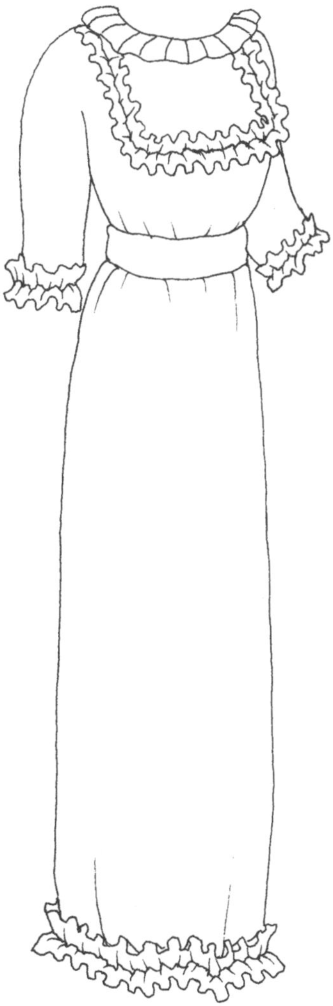

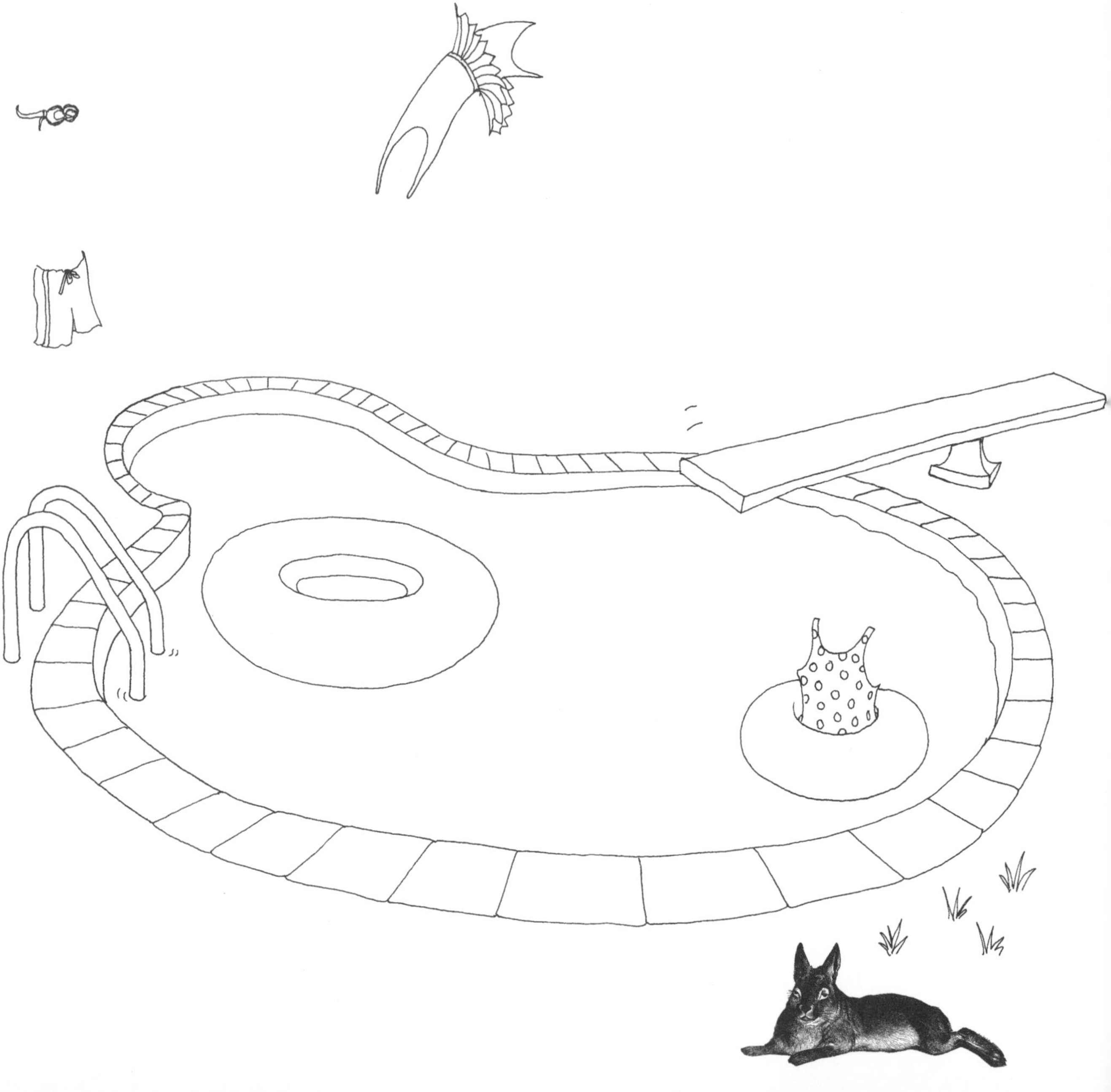

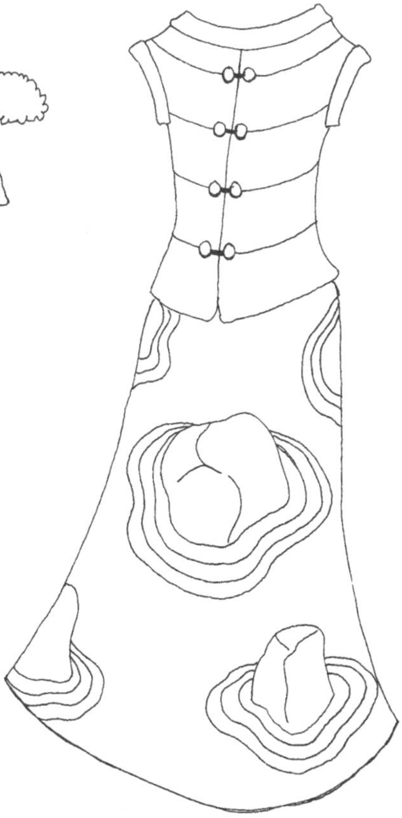
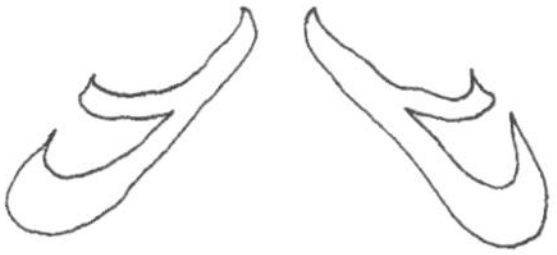

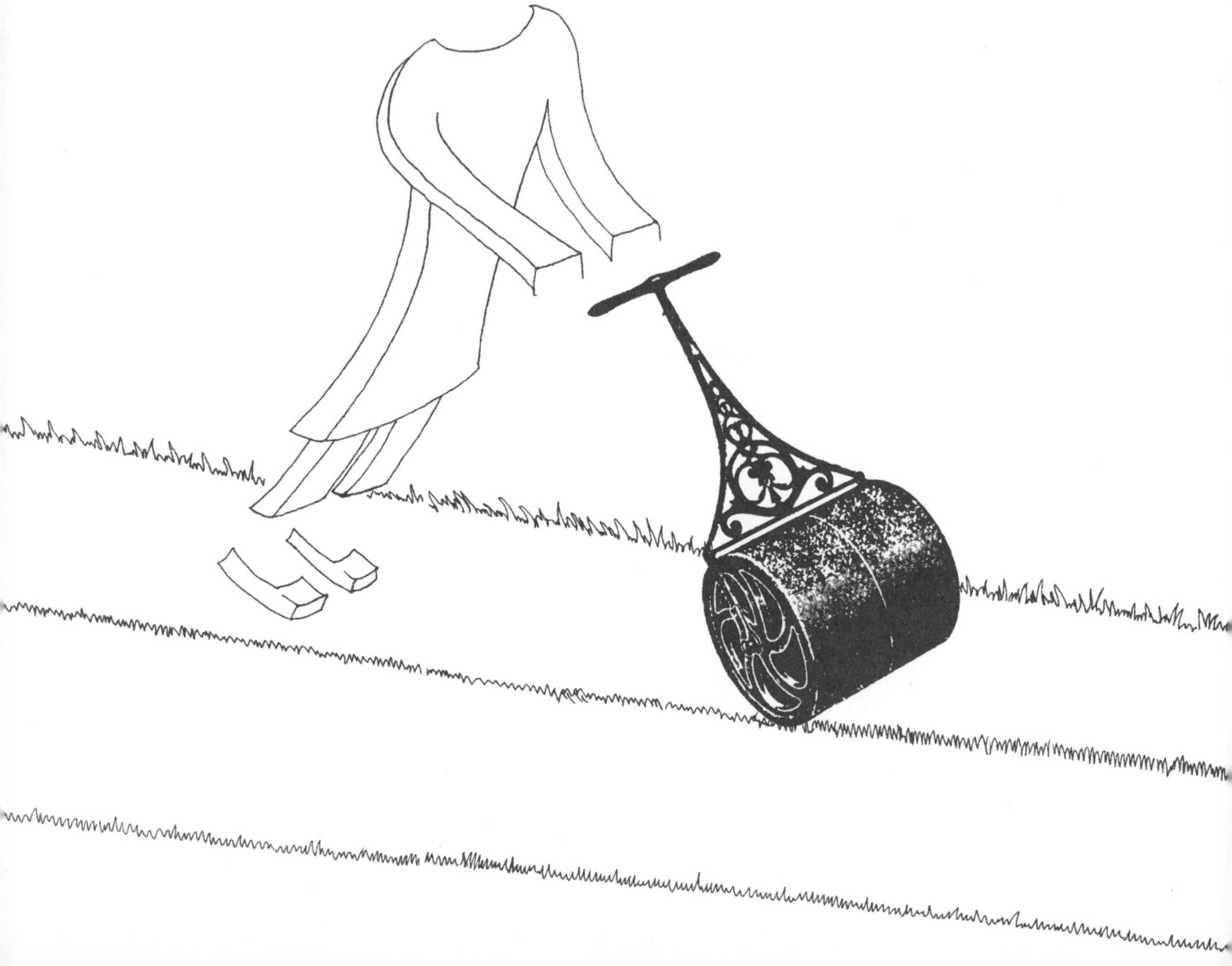

Another postcard for
you to color and mail.

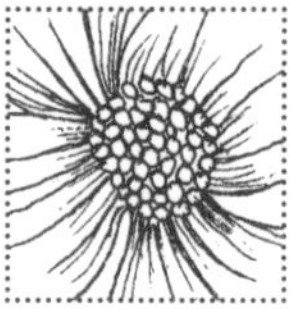